Genre Narrative N[...]

MW00570031

 Essential Question
Why do we need government?

A DAY IN THE SENATE

by **TERRY MILLER SHANNON**

Chapter 1

MEET A SENATOR

You might not think that senators have much to do with people like you. However, what they do affects you and everyone else in the country.

Senators make laws that shape things in your everyday life. They pass laws that set the speed limits on the highways. They decide if a new interstate will be built in your town.

Senators work in the **Senate**. The Senate and the **House of Representatives** make up **Congress**. Congress is the legislative, or lawmaking, branch of the U.S. government.

We need legislation, or laws, to help the country run smoothly. Laws give us rules to follow. Without them, everyday life would be chaotic.

Senators work in the Capitol building in Washington, D.C.

A candidate campaigns across the state to try to win a seat in the Senate.

Sometimes new laws are needed to solve problems. Sometimes existing laws need to change to make them work better. Senators study problems and work with other lawmakers to turn the best solutions into laws.

People choose senators by voting in elections. Two senators represent each state in the Senate.

Let's look at what happens during a day in the Senate.

Who Can Become a Senator?

A senator must be at least 30 years old and live in the state he or she represents. A senator also must be a United States citizen for at least nine years before being elected.

Each senator's **term** lasts for six years. When a senator is elected, he or she makes a commitment to serve the full term.

Many senators begin their day by meeting with their staff. All senators need a good team of people to help them. It would be impossible to do a good job without help.

Staffers, the people who work for the senators, arrange meetings for the senators. They make sure the senators know where to be and what they need to do.

Staffers perform many other tasks as well. If the Senate is discussing a new highway project, a senator needs information about it. The senator needs to know how it will be paid for. He or she needs to know how it will affect people living nearby. Staffers find answers to these questions.

U.S. Capitol Map

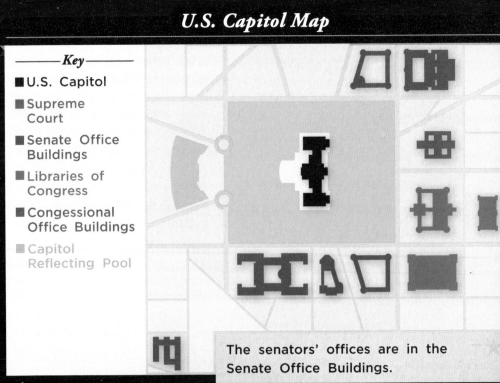

——— Key ———

■ U.S. Capitol

■ Supreme Court

■ Senate Office Buildings

■ Libraries of Congress

■ Congessional Office Buildings

■ Capitol Reflecting Pool

The senators' offices are in the Senate Office Buildings.

Staffers for Senator Olympia Snowe of Maine (far left) do many jobs to help her.

At their staff meetings, senators and staffers talk about what's on the calendar for the day. On a typical day, most senators attend several **committee** meetings. Much of the Senate's work is done in small groups called committees.

Every committee works on a different subject. Some committees study education issues, while others work on budgets. Each committee has senators from different states.

WORKING TOGETHER

After the staff meeting, a senator might head to the Capitol building for a committee meeting. Senators can ride the Capitol subway to get there.

Senators work together in committee meetings to study new bills. A bill is a proposed law that has not been passed by Congress yet.

For example, the education committee might meet to discuss a bill that recommends reducing the size of all kindergarten to third-grade classrooms to only 18 students.

A subway connects the Capitol to other buildings.

Supporters of the bill argue that smaller classes improve students' reading skills. If the bill becomes law, more teachers will need to be trained and hired.

The committee asks government agencies, such as the Department of Education, for more information about the subject. Senators also invite education experts to talk. The experts give the committee information about the connection between class size and reading ability.

After gathering more information, the committee might decide to leave the bill as it is. It might add amendments, or changes, to the bill.

The committee will then vote on whether to send the completed bill to the full Senate. There, all of the senators can discuss the bill.

Senator Scott Brown asks a question during a committee meeting.

Committee meetings last for different amounts of time. All meetings break for lunch, though. Fortunately, senators don't have to go far to find a restaurant.

The Capitol and its office buildings are truly a city within a city. They contain cafeterias and a gym. There are even a beauty parlor, a dry cleaner, and a barbershop!

Having so many resources in the Capitol and the office buildings saves lawmakers time.

A view of the Capitol in 1856 after the dome had been removed.

In 1793, building of the Capitol began. President George Washington laid the cornerstone on September 18, 1793. Builders finished the Senate wing in 1800.

During the War of 1812, British soldiers set fire to the Capitol. Luckily, the building wasn't completely destroyed. Once it was repaired, the building held the Senate, the House of Representatives, and the Supreme Court. By 1850, the Capitol was already too small for the senators and representatives.

The Capitol was extended in the 1850s. The dome was taken down and replaced with a new dome.

Today the Capitol covers an area of 175,170 square feet. Today, the House of Representatives and the Senate meet in the Capitol building.

A SENATE VOTE

After lunch, senators might meet in the **Senate Chamber** to discuss legislation and to vote on completed bills. Visitors can watch from a gallery above.

Senators have the privilege of speech and debate. This means that they can speak freely in the chamber. This rule allows them to better represent the people in their state.

Senate Pages

Pages deliver messages and other documents in the Senate. They also prepare the Chamber for Senate sessions. A page must be a high school junior who is at least 16 years old.

Pages go to school in the morning at the United States Senate Page School. Then they watch history in the making while they work at the Capitol.

Ingram Publishing/SuperStock

When a bill is up for a vote, a Senate officer records each senator's vote. The vote also shows up on a screen on the wall above the Senate Gallery.

After a bill is approved in the Senate or the House of Representatives, it must go to the other house to be voted on and passed. In other words, either house of Congress can suggest bills, but both houses must approve the final bill.

Sometimes the Senate and the House of Representatives cannot agree on everything in the bill. In these cases, they form a joint committee to resolve their differences.

This page got to meet President Obama.

Bills often go through many changes. This happens because people have different points of view. All the people involved might need to compromise, or accept some changes, so that the bill will be approved. This means that the final law might be a very different version of the bill that was first proposed.

After the Senate and the House or Representatives have approved a bill, it is sent to the president. When the president signs the bill, it becomes a law. The president can veto, or refuse to sign a bill.

Compromise is necessary
for most bills to be passed.

Visitors can watch the senators at work from the Senate Gallery.

Another important part of a senator's day is meeting with **constituents**, or people from their home states. Staffers organize these meetings, which give constituents a chance to ask questions and to share their ideas or concerns.

Many school groups visit their senators to see Congress at work. They can visit the Exhibition Hall, which has displays about the history of Congress. They also might visit the Senate Chamber. Here they can watch the activity on the floor from the Senate Gallery.

Senators work long hours. They usually travel a lot. At the end of a day, a senator might fly back to his or her home state.

Every senator has an office back home in the state he or she represents. Here senators meet with more of their constituents to listen to their concerns. This is how the senator stays in touch with voters and their issues. It is how those issues make their way to Washington, D.C., and eventually make their way into law.

(c) Kerry-Edwards 2004, Inc./Sharon Farmer, photographer. (bl) Wetzel and Company

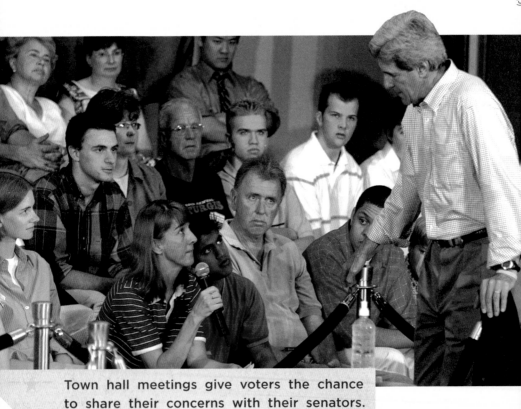

Town hall meetings give voters the chance to share their concerns with their senators.

Respond to Reading

Summarize

Use key details from *A Day in the Senate* to summarize the selection. Your graphic organizer may help you.

Cause → Effect
→
→
→
→

Text Evidence

1. What features in *A Day in the Senate* help you identify it as informational text? GENRE

2. Reread page 7. If a committee agrees on a bill, what happens as a result? CAUSE AND EFFECT

3. The word *elections* on page 3 contains the Latin root *lect*, which means "to choose." What does *elections* mean? Explain how context clues and knowing the root helped you. LATIN ROOTS

4. Write about why bills change before they become laws. WRITE ABOUT READING

Compare Texts

Read about Inauguration Day, when a new president's term begins.

A New President Takes Office

The United States is a democracy, which means it is governed by the people. The president leads the country's people.

The Constitution has rules about how people elect a president. A presidential election is held every four years. The winner usually takes office on January 20.

The day the new president takes office is called Inauguration Day. It takes place in Washington, D.C., in front of the Capitol.

President Barack Obama took the oath of office on January 20, 2009.

(t and b) Ingram Publishing/SuperStock, (bl) Jae C. Hong/AP/CORBIS

More than a million people may watch a presidential inauguration.

Inauguration Day is filled with tradition. The new president takes the **oath** of office. He or she officially becomes the president the moment the oath is said.

The oath's words are in the Constitution: "I do solemnly swear that I will faithfully execute the office of President of the United States, and will to the best of my ability, preserve, protect and defend the Constitution of the United States."

The president takes the oath of office at noon. Afterward, the new president gives a speech called the inaugural address.

In their inauguration speeches, presidents state their goals for the nation. On March 4, 1861, Abraham Lincoln aimed his inauguration speech at the southern states. He said, "... no State upon its own mere motion can lawfully get out of the Union ... You have no oath registered in heaven to destroy the Government, while I shall have the most solemn one to preserve, protect, and defend it."

At the time, some southern states were trying to break away from the United States. President Lincoln was telling them that he would do anything to save the union and to keep the country together.

This illustration shows Abraham Lincoln taking the oath of office.

Make Connections

Why is Inauguration Day held? ESSENTIAL QUESTION

Compare the role of a senator in *A Day in the Senate* with the role of a president in *A New President Takes Office*. TEXT TO TEXT

Glossary

committee *(kuh-MI-tee)* a small group of lawmakers who consider bills in a specific area *(page 5)*

Congress *(KON-gruhs)* the legislative branch of the U.S. government, consisting of the Senate and the House of Representatives *(page 2)*

constituents *(kuhn-STICH-yew-wuhnts)* people who live in an elected official's home state or Congressional district *(page 13)*

House of Representatives *(HOWS uhv re-pri-ZEN-tuh-tivz)* one house of Congress; works with the Senate to write and pass the country's laws *(page 2)*

oath *(ohth)* a solemn promise *(page 17)*

Senate *(SE-nuht)* one house of Congress; works with the House of Representatives to write and pass the country's laws *(page 2)*

Senate Chamber *(SE-nuht CHAYM-buhr)* the room in which senators meet to debate and vote on laws *(page 10)*

term *(turm)* the period for which a senator or other elected official serves *(page 3)*

Index

Focus on
Social Studies

Purpose To find out why people run for public office

Procedure

Step 1 With a partner or in a small group, make a list of your local school board members. You can find this online or ask at the school office.

Step 2 Write a short letter or e-mail to each elected board member, asking him or her to say, in 50 words or fewer, why he or she ran for office. Show your letter or e-mail to your teacher before you send it. Make sure that each board member receives only one letter or e-mail.

Step 3 With your group, analyze the responses you receive. Make a chart or graph to show the results. Display the results and discuss them with the class.

Step 4 Write another letter or e-mail to the school board members who responded, thanking them for their help.